Feel
Good
Smoothies

Feel
Good
Smoothies

40 Smoothies to Power
Your Body and Mind

Sandra Wu

Illustrations by **Rocío Egío**

CHRONICLE BOOKS

SAN FRANCISCO

Library of Congress Cataloging-in-Publication Data available.

ISBN 978-1-7972-1059-9

Manufactured in China.

Illustrations by Rocío Egío.
Design by Lizzie Vaughan.

Typeset in Gotham and Frito Vandito.

10 9 8 7 6 5 4 3 2 1

Chronicle books and gifts are available at special quantity discounts to corporations, professional associations, literacy programs, and other organizations. For details and discount information, please contact our premiums department at corporatesales@chroniclebooks.com or at 1-800-759-0190.

Chronicle Books LLC
680 Second Street
San Francisco, California 94107
www.chroniclebooks.com

CONTENTS

Wake-Up Blends

Chock-Full o' Berries

Introduction

There's nothing easier than whipping up a delicious smoothie. And even better, it's a foolproof way to get the vital nutrients your body needs in a drinkable, no-fuss meal. This book takes the casual approach to smoothies—there's no need to buy any crazy supplements, powders, or mixes. Every drink featured here relies on the magical flavors and health benefits of ingredients you can find in any grocery store or specialty market. Just as diverse as you'd want any meal to be, these smoothies tap into different moods and moments of your day to suit your needs. From perfect breakfast boosts to relaxing tropical blends, post-workout cooling drinks, and treat-yourself desserts without the guilt, there are endless ways to sip your way to feeling good. As you flip through these pages for smoothie inspiration, you'll notice each recipe has a little badge that indicates its main benefit: Digestion, Relax, Energy, Immunity, and more. Also included is a handy guide to the main ingredients found in this collection so you can build up your blending skills and imagine up your own drinks.

recipes in this book · SERVE 2 · unless otherwise noted

Smoothie Ingredient Guide

Here you'll find a quick guide to most of the ingredients featured in this book, as well as their main health benefits. Let it inspire you to create your own blended concoctions!

FRUIT/VEGETABLE	WHAT'S IN IT	HOW IT CAN HELP
Acai	Fiber, minerals, vitamin A	Improves immunity and memory
Avocado	Fiber, monounsaturated fats, potassium, vitamins B_6, C, and K	Lowers blood pressure; supports eye, gut, and heart health
Banana	Fiber, potassium, vitamins B_6 and C	Boosts mood, supports gut and heart health
Beet	Antioxidants, dietary nitrates, magnesium, vitamin B_9	Aids digestion, lowers blood pressure, supports heart health
Blackberry	Fiber, vitamins C and K	Aids digestion, supports brain and dental health
Blueberry	Antioxidants, fiber, manganese, vitamins C and K	Helps with aging, improves immunity, supports brain and muscle health
Cantaloupe	Fiber; potassium; vitamins A, B_9, and C; water	Hydrates, improves immunity, reduces colds, supports eye health

Celery	Iron; magnesium; sodium; vitamins A, C, and K	Aids digestion, lowers blood pressure
Corn	Fiber; vitamins B_1, B_9, and C	Aids digestion
Cucumber	Potassium, vitamins C and K, water	Hydrates, supports bone and heart health
Dragon Fruit	Antioxidants, fiber, magnesium	Improves immunity, lowers blood sugar
Fig	Copper, vitamin B_6	Energizes, supports brain health
Goji Berry	Antioxidants; copper; iron; vitamins A, B_2, and C	Energizes, helps with aging, improves immunity, supports heart health
Grape	Vitamins C and K	Boosts mood; energizes; supports bone, eye, and heart health
Grapefruit	Antioxidants, vitamins A and C	Hydrates, improves immunity, supports heart health
Honeydew	Potassium; vitamins B_6, C, and K; water	Hydrates, supports bone and skin health
Kale	Calcium; copper; manganese; potassium; vitamins A, B_6, C, and K	Boosts mood, helps with aging, improves immunity, supports bone and heart health
Kiwi	Potassium; vitamins B_9, C, E, and K	Aids digestion, improves immunity, supports eye and lung health
Lychee	Copper, potassium, vitamin C	Improves immunity, supports heart health

FRUIT/VEGETABLE	WHAT'S IN IT	HOW IT CAN HELP
Mango	Antioxidants; copper; fiber; vitamins A, B_6, B_9, C, and E	Aids digestion; improves immunity; supports eye, hair, heart, and skin health
Mint	Fiber, iron, vitamin A	Improves digestion, supports eye health
Orange	Antioxidants; fiber; potassium; vitamins B_1, B_9, and C	Aids digestion, improves immunity, supports heart health
Papaya	Antioxidants; fiber; vitamins A, B_9, and C	Aids digestion, improves immunity, supports heart and skin health
Peach	Antioxidants; copper; fiber; vitamins A, C, E, and K	Aids digestion, supports heart and skin health
Pear	Copper, fiber, potassium, vitamins C and K	Energizes; supports heart, gut, and skin health
Persimmon	Copper; fiber; manganese; vitamins A, B_6, C, E, and K	Aids digestion, improves immunity, supports eye and heart health
Pineapple	Copper; fiber; manganese; vitamins B_6, B_9, and C	Aids digestion, energizes, improves immunity
Plum/Prune	Fiber; vitamins A, B_2, B_3, B_6, and K	Aids digestion, supports bone and heart health
Pumpkin	Fiber; iron; potassium; vitamins A, B_2, C, and E	Aids digestion; improves immunity; supports eye, heart, and skin health
Raspberry	Fiber; magnesium; vitamins B, C, E, and K	Helps with aging, improves immunity

Spinach	Calcium; fiber; iron; vitamins A, B_9, C, and K	Improves immunity; supports bone, eye, and skin health
Strawberry	Antioxidants; fiber; potassium; vitamins B_9 and C	Improves immunity; supports heart and skin health
Sweet Potato	Antioxidants; copper; fiber; potassium; vitamins A, B_6, and C	Improves immunity; supports brain, eye, and gut health
Watermelon	Copper; potassium; vitamins A, B_5, and C; water	Hydrates, improves immunity, supports heart and skin health

Smoothie Pantry

Some of the ingredients featured in this book may or may not be familiar to you. This handy pantry reference will help you navigate through the health food aisles, bulk bins, and specialty stores with ease.

ALMONDS (BUTTER, MILK, WHOLE)

Almonds are a powerhouse ingredient, packed with protein, antioxidants, and other essential vitamins and minerals. When buying the butter and milk versions, look for brands that use a minimal amount of additives, beyond ones for improving nutrition.

BEE POLLEN

Bee pollen is collected by placing small brushes on the entrance of a beehive, gently collecting a portion of the pollen. Bee pollen has been shown to help combat seasonal allergies, so be sure to buy local and from a trusted beekeeper/producer.

BROWN RICE

By retaining more of its outer layers compared to its fully shelled white version, brown rice is an excellent source of fiber. Because it takes longer to cook than other types of rice, try making a big batch and sealing extra in an airtight container. It can be stored in the freezer for up to 6 months.

CACAO (POWDER, NIBS)

Cultivated from cacao beans, this is a healthier way to enjoy a chocolate-like flavor. Never replace cacao powder with cocoa powder, which is more highly processed and roasted at a higher temperature.

CASHEWS

Compared to other nuts, cashews are relatively soft and sweeter in texture and taste. Make sure to store cashews in an airtight container and discard any shriveled-looking ones you may find.

CHIA SEEDS

Chia seeds, an edible seed loaded with antioxidants, come in two varieties: white and black. There is very little nutritional difference between the two, so choose whichever brand has the best quality seeds and value.

CHICKPEAS

Rich in fiber and protein, chickpeas are an easy way to add in lots of nutrients. The cooking time from raw to cooked chickpeas is a long one, so if you're pressed for time, opt for the canned variety (just watch for sodium levels).

COCONUT MILK

Rich and creamy in consistency, reach for coconut milk when you want a punch of coconut flavor. Just be sure to use it in moderation because a little can go a long way in flavor.

COCONUT MILK BEVERAGE

While shopping for this creamy healthy fat, be sure to choose the cartons in the refrigerated case or the shelf-stable variety packed in aseptic boxes next to the alternative milk products; those tend to be much lower in saturated fat and calories than the traditional canned variety and are much more drinkable.

COCONUT WATER

Super drinkable and full of electrolytes, coconut water is the ultimate way to rehydrate. Be sure to pick up products that have the least amount of processing (e.g., added sugars or "natural flavors").

DATES

Medjool dates, cultivated in California, are the ideal variety

for smoothie mak-
ing, in that they tend
to be softer than the
imported versions and
thus easier to blend.

FLAXSEED MEAL
A gut's best friend,
flaxseed has lots of
fiber and omega-3
fatty acids. The ground
meal, rather than whole
flaxseeds, makes it
easier to digest and
absorb its nutrients.
However, if you have a
coffee grinder at home,
buy the whole seeds
and grind up what you
need in that moment to
retain freshness.

HEMP HEARTS
For a heart-healthy
boost and a good
source of magnesium,
hemp hearts are hard
to beat. Hemp hearts
are ideal compared to
hemp seeds, which are
the unshelled version.

HIBISCUS TEA
This deep-red tea is
rich in antioxidants. If
you're making the tea
fresh from home, try
to find teas that use
larger pieces of hibiscus
(rather than powdered
versions).

MACA POWDER
Nutty in taste, this pow-
der has been known to
be a great mood and
energy booster. Be sure
to purchase products
sourced only from Peru,
where it's native, for the
best quality.

MATCHA POWDER
This powdered green
tea has numerous
potential benefits,
including possible
cancer-fighting prop-
erties. Look for matcha
that is bright green in
color and has a pro-
nounced vegetal smell,
which indicates better
quality.

OATS (MILK, ROLLED)
Oats are rich in fiber
and a quality break-
fast staple. The rolled
version, compared
to steel-cut, are ideal
for smoothie making
because they tend to
be creamier in texture
while still retaining lots
of health benefits.

SOY MILK

Soy is a great option for protein for the dairy-averse. As with other nondairy milks, try to choose brands that have a shorter ingredient list, to avoid unnecessary additives.

SPIRULINA POWDER

This nutrient-dense blue-green algae is packed with protein, vitamins, minerals, carotenoids, and antioxidants. Look for spirulina products with a deep, dark green color.

TAHINI

Tahini is a creamy and savory way to add in healthy fats. Oil separating from tahini in the container is normal, but you should try to stir it occasionally to prevent it from separating entirely, at which point it will become too hard to reconstitute.

TOFU

Tofu is an amazing source of protein, and it contains all the essential amino acids you need. Because soybeans tend to be GMO, try to buy organic tofu when possible.

TURMERIC

This anti-inflammatory and antioxidant power-house is best taken with black pepper, which helps the body absorb its nutrients. Like most ingredients, opt for organic, so you can ensure a purer and higher-quality product.

YOGURT

Yogurt is an ideal way to help regulate your gut health, thanks to the incredible amount of probiotics found in it. Greek yogurt is going to be thicker in consistency and may also be a better alternative for those who are lactose intolerant, because of the straining process.

Smoothie Making

 INVEST IN A HIGH-PERFORMANCE BLENDER. It might be a pricier buy but a worthy investment that will last years (and thousands of smoothies).

 PORTION OUT YOUR INGREDIENTS in advance and store them in the freezer for quick assembly.

 USE CHILLED INGREDIENTS whenever possible.

 FREEZE HALF OF THE LIQUID you're using if you want a more frozen, milkshake-like consistency.

 BE SURE TO ADD THE INGREDIENTS IN THE ORDER that they're listed in the recipe to ensure everything gets blended properly.

 USE A BLENDER TAMPER to aid in stirring stubborn ingredients while blending. If you can't get your hands on one, turning off the blender and using a stiff spatula as needed will help with thicker smoothies.

YOU CAN STORE PREMADE SMOOTHIES in an airtight container in the fridge for up to 1 day or in the freezer for up to 2 months. Before enjoying a frozen smoothie, simply let it melt a little to your preferred consistency.

MAKE IT A SMOOTHIE BOWL: Place your smoothie in a bowl and top with your favorite sliced fresh and/ or dried fruit. If your smoothie is a little too loose for a bowl, place it in the freezer for about 10 minutes to thicken it up.

SMOOTHIE BOWL TOPPING IDEAS: Dried coconut shreds, banana slices, chia seeds, blueberries, strawberry slices, honey, bee pollen.

Menus

Looking for a smoothie recipe to help with something specific? Check out the menus below.

MOOD

RELAX

Wake-Up Blends

Hearty and satisfying, these smoothies are perfect for starting a lazy Sunday or whipping up as an on-the-go breakfast.

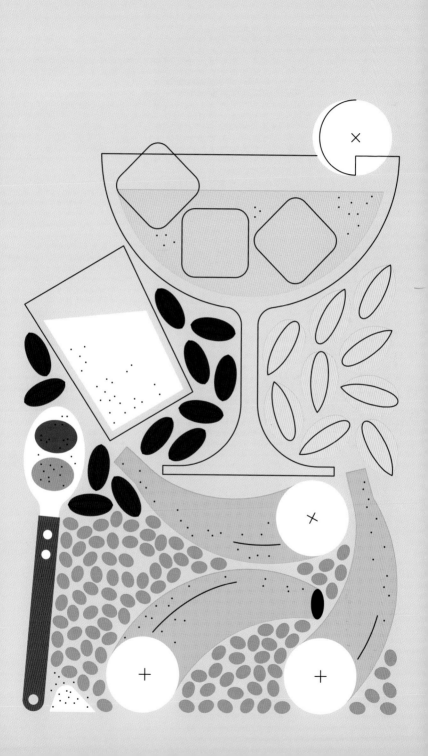

Brown Rice Horchata

1 cup [135 g] frozen banana slices

1 cup [240 ml] plain unsweetened almond milk

½ cup [60 g] cooked brown rice, chilled

¼ cup [25 g] sliced almonds

2 Tbsp raisins

¼ tsp cinnamon

¼ tsp vanilla extract

Pinch of sea salt

¼ cup [45 g] ice cubes

DIGESTION

Evoking the beloved Mexican drink, this creamy smoothie is just the thing for a hot day. Rich in fiber and essential nutrients (including a boost of potassium from the bananas), this smoothie is a tummy's best friend. If you want to get extra decadent (really, who doesn't?), rim the edge of your serving glass with an equal-parts mixture of cinnamon and sugar before pouring in the smoothie.

Make it

Place the banana, almond milk, rice, almonds, raisins, cinnamon, vanilla, salt, and ice in a blender. Start the blender on low speed and slowly increase to high speed. Blend until smooth and creamy.

Chai Breakfast

¾ cup [180 ml] brewed unsweetened chai tea

½ cup [120 ml] plain unsweetened oat milk

¼ cup [25 g] old-fashioned rolled oats

1 medium banana, peeled, sliced, and frozen

¼ cup [30 g] walnut pieces, toasted
and cooled completely

2 tsp honey

Pinch of sea salt

ENERGY

For a spice-filled boost of energy, try making this heart-healthy smoothie. For the best flavor, make the tea using a loose-leaf blend or tea bag, not chai concentrate, and do not sweeten or add milk—the honey and oat milk provide all the sweetness and creaminess you adore in a chai tea. Note: You'll need to start this smoothie recipe the night before.

Make it

In a medium bowl, combine the chai, oat milk, and oats. Cover and refrigerate overnight.

Place the soaked oat mixture, banana, walnuts, honey, and salt in a blender. Start the blender on low speed and slowly increase to high speed. Blend until smooth and creamy.

Chocolate Almond Butter Cup

¾ cup [180 ml] plain unsweetened almond milk

½ cup [80 g] cooked chickpeas

½ cup [10 g] packed baby spinach

5 pitted Medjool dates

2 Tbsp almond butter

2 Tbsp raw cacao powder

Pinch of sea salt

½ cup [85 g] ice cubes

MUSCLE
BOOST

Not only is this smoothie a delicious and decadent way to enjoy chocolate, but it's also a smart way to get in some essential nutrients, such as protein and antioxidants, thanks to chickpeas, almond butter, and raw cacao powder.

Make it

Place the almond milk, chickpeas, spinach, dates, almond butter, cacao powder, salt, and ice in a blender. Start the blender on low speed and slowly increase to high speed. Blend until smooth and creamy.

Hazelnut Mocha Shake

2 medium bananas, peeled, sliced, and frozen

¾ cup [180 ml] brewed coffee, chilled

¼ cup [30 g] whole hazelnuts, toasted and cooled completely

¼ cup [30 g] cacao nibs

Pinch of sea salt

ENERGY

This pick-me-up smoothie is a great morning choice for keeping you full and alert longer than a cup of coffee ever could. It may also help with your morning blues: Cacao nibs, made from crushed cacao beans, may act as a mood enhancer thanks to compounds that increase the brain's levels of endorphins and serotonin.

Make it

Place the bananas, coffee, hazelnuts, cacao nibs, and salt in a blender. Start the blender on low speed and slowly increase to high speed. Blend until smooth and creamy.

Matcha Avocado Frappé

¾ cup [180 ml] plain unsweetened almond milk

2 kale leaves, stems removed and leaves roughly torn

¼ medium Hass avocado, peeled and pitted

5 pitted Medjool dates

1½ tsp matcha powder

Pinch of sea salt

1 cup [160 g] ice cubes

ENERGY

Matcha is a health powerhouse: Not only does it provide a tasty caffeine boost, it also contains a group of antioxidants called catechins, believed to have cancer-fighting effects, and the stress-reducing amino acid L-theanine. Add in fatty-for-all-the-right-reasons avocado, and you've got a dream breakfast.

Make it

Place the almond milk, kale, avocado, dates, matcha, salt, and ice in a blender. Start the blender on low speed and slowly increase to high speed. Blend until smooth and creamy.

PB&J

1 cup [240 ml] plain unsweetened oat milk

⅓ cup [30 g] old-fashioned rolled oats

1 cup [160 g] frozen seedless red grapes

2 Tbsp peanut butter

1 tsp maple syrup

Pinch of sea salt

HEARTY

Inspired by the nostalgic after-school lunch, this drink is designed to keep you full in a sustainable way. Peanut butter is a fantastic source of mono-unsaturated fats and protein, and combined with fiber-rich rolled oats, this smoothie is super satisfying. Note: You'll need to start this smoothie recipe the night before.

Make it

In a medium bowl, combine the oat milk and oats. Cover and refrigerate overnight.

Place the soaked oat mixture, grapes, peanut butter, maple syrup, and salt in a blender. Start the blender on low speed and slowly increase to high speed. Blend until smooth and creamy.

Pear Oatmeal Breakfast Smoothie

1 cup [240 ml] plain unsweetened almond milk

¼ cup [25 g] old-fashioned rolled oats

1 ripe Bartlett or d'Anjou pear, cored, chopped, and frozen

1 Tbsp flaxseed meal

1 Tbsp maple syrup

1 Tbsp almond butter

⅛ tsp cinnamon

Pinch of sea salt

DIGESTION

Try this nourishing blend when you're looking to add more fiber and vitamin C. The cinnamon notes make it a versatile base for a smoothie bowl—just top with bananas, chia seeds, or any of your favorite toppings. Note: You'll need to start this recipe the night before.

Make it

In a medium bowl, combine the almond milk and oats. Cover and refrigerate overnight.

Place the oat mixture, pear, flaxseed meal, maple syrup, almond butter, cinnamon, and salt in a blender. Start on low speed and slowly increase to high speed. Blend until smooth and creamy.

Green Milkshake

1½ cups [360 ml] plain unsweetened almond milk

½ medium Hass avocado, peeled and pitted

½ medium banana, peeled, sliced, and frozen

¼ cup [5 g] frozen spinach

2 tsp maple syrup

2 tsp maca powder

Pinch of sea salt

MUSCLE BOOST

This ultra-thick and creamy green smoothie has a consistency similar to a milkshake, but it's light-years healthier than the soda shop treat. The saturated fats in ice cream's main ingredients, heavy cream and egg yolks, are replaced here with the mostly monounsaturated fats of the avocado.

Make it

Place the almond milk, avocado, banana, spinach, maple syrup, maca powder, and salt in a blender. Start the blender on low speed and slowly increase to high speed. Blend until smooth and creamy.

Chock-Full o' Berries

These smoothies feature immunity-strengthening, memory-boosting berries, such as blueberries, cranberries, strawberries, and others. Blend up one of these before a study session, at the start of the workweek, or whenever you need a little healthy nudge.

Acai Blackberry Fusion

1 cup [120 g] frozen blackberries

½ cup [120 g] plain whole-milk yogurt

½ cup [120 ml] orange juice

One 3½ oz [100 g] packet frozen acai purée

1 Tbsp manuka honey

Pinch of sea salt

IMMUNITY

This deep purple smoothie is sweetened with a magical ingredient: manuka honey. Cultivated in New Zealand, manuka honey is known to have naturally antibacterial properties. You can find it at health food stores. Look for products with 15+ unique manuka factor (UMF) or more.

Make it

Place the blackberries, yogurt, orange juice, acai purée, honey, and salt in a blender. Start the blender on low speed and slowly increase to high speed. Blend until smooth and creamy.

Beets and Berries

¾ cup [105 g] frozen mixed berries

½ cup [105 g] peeled and diced cooked beets

½ cup [80 g] frozen blood orange segments

½ cup [120 ml] unsweetened pomegranate juice

Pinch of sea salt

Sweet and just the right amount of tart, this smoothie is a bit sneaky in that a healthy amount of berries and memory-boosting pomegranate juice hide a powerhouse ingredient: beets. Although their distinctive taste can be a bit overpowering, beets' presence in this blend are well worth it, thanks to their high levels of antioxidants, vitamin C, and fiber.

Make it

Place the berries, beets, blood orange segments, pomegranate juice, and salt in a blender. Start the blender on low speed and slowly increase to high speed. Blend until smooth and creamy.

Cranberry Orange Harvest

1 navel orange, peeled, segmented, and frozen (about ¾ cup [95 g])

½ cup [70 g] frozen banana slices

½ cup [60 g] diced skin-on sweet red apple, such as Fuji or Gala

¾ cup [180 ml] unsweetened cranberry juice

2 Tbsp flaxseed meal

2 tsp honey

Pinch of sea salt

IMMUNITY

Make sure to use unsweetened cranberry juice, not overly sweet cranberry juice cocktail, for this drink. A combination of apples, banana, and honey work to temper the tartness of the antioxidant-packed cranberry juice.

Make it

Place the orange segments, banana, apple, cranberry juice, flaxseed meal, honey, and salt in a blender. Start the blender on low speed and slowly increase to high speed. Blend until smooth and creamy.

Kiwi Strawberry Delight

1 cup [250 g] silken tofu

½ cup [70 g] frozen quartered strawberries

2 golden kiwis, peeled, halved, and frozen

2 tsp honey

Pinch of sea salt

If you can score some at your local produce store, golden kiwis (rather than the more popular green variety) are worth the search. They tend to be naturally sweeter and more fragrant. Plus, their high quantities of fiber, vitamin C (three times more than an orange), vitamin E, and potassium can't hurt.

Make it

Place the tofu, strawberries, kiwis, honey, and salt in a blender. Start the blender on low speed and slowly increase to high speed. Blend until smooth and creamy.

IMMUNITY

Land of Figs and Honey

REPAIR

1 cup [120 g] frozen raspberries

4 Black Mission figs

¾ cup [180 ml] orange juice

½ cup [120 g] plain whole-milk yogurt

2 tsp honey

¼ tsp vanilla extract

Pinch of sea salt

Creamy, sweet, and tart, this smoothie is ideal for a pre- or post-workout meal. It's loaded with figs, which naturally contain calcium, magnesium, and potassium, contributing to strong bones.

Make it

Place the raspberries, figs, orange juice, yogurt, honey, vanilla, and salt in a blender. Start the blender on low speed and slowly increase to high speed. Blend until smooth and creamy.

Mixed Berry Goji Plus

1¼ cups [175 g] frozen mixed berries

2 Tbsp goji berries

1 cup [240 g] plain whole-milk yogurt

1 tsp maple syrup

Pinch of sea salt

1 Tbsp chia seeds

IMMUNITY

Little goji berries really pack a lot into such a small package: Loaded with antioxidants and lots of vitamin C, they add to this immunity-boosting smoothie. Turn to this drink for an easy and flavorful way to prepare for the flu and cold season (which, honestly, is any time). Be sure to add the chia seeds near the end so they stay intact and suspended within the drink.

Make it

Place the mixed berries, goji berries, yogurt, maple syrup, and salt in a blender. Start the blender on low speed and slowly increase to high speed. Blend until smooth and creamy. Add the chia seeds and blend on medium speed to combine.

Nectarine Blueberry Buttermilk

1 cup [240 ml] buttermilk

1 cup [130 g] frozen nectarine slices

¼ cup [35 g] frozen blueberries

¼ cup [80 g] hemp hearts

1 Tbsp honey

Pinch of sea salt

REPAIR

It sounds like an unusual smoothie ingredient, but buttermilk is a handy addition to this cooling drink. A good source of both calcium and probiotics, it's easier to digest than regular milk because it has less lactose.

Make it

Place the buttermilk, nectarine slices, blueberries, hemp hearts, honey, and salt in a blender. Start the blender on low speed and slowly increase to high speed. Blend until smooth and creamy.

Pink Grapefruit Pom-Pom

1 cup [240 ml] unsweetened pomegranate juice

1 medium pink grapefruit, peeled, segmented, and frozen (about 1 cup [130 g])

½ cup [70 g] frozen quartered strawberries

1 tsp honey

½ tsp grated fresh ginger

Pinch of sea salt

Feeling not your best after some questionable food choices or a long night out on the town? Try out this blend. Long used as a home remedy for a variety of ailments, ginger is a calming force for sour stomachs.

Make it

Place the pomegranate juice, grapefruit, strawberries, honey, ginger, and salt in a blender. Start the blender on low speed and slowly increase to high speed. Blend until smooth and creamy.

REPAIR

Strawberry Blush

1 cup [140 g] frozen quartered strawberries

1 cup [240 ml] whole milk

1 Tbsp fresh lemon juice

1 Tbsp honey

⅛ tsp rosewater

Pinch of sea salt

2 Tbsp chia seeds

RELAX

Soothing rosewater gives this blend a calming, aromatic quality that helps you relax. And as an added bonus, rosewater naturally contains antioxidants, so both body and mind can feel at ease.

Make it

Place the strawberries, milk, lemon juice, honey, rosewater, and salt in a blender. Start the blender on low speed and slowly increase to high speed. Blend until smooth and creamy. Add the chia seeds and blend on medium speed to combine.

Tropical Sippers

Easy, breezy, and refreshing, these vitamin C–rich smoothies are ideal for unwinding and enjoying a midday treat.

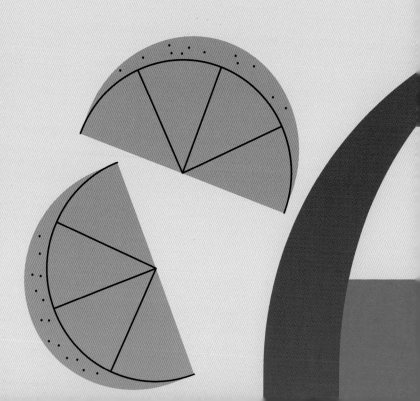

Hibiscus Cantaloupe Blend

½ cup [120 ml] brewed hibiscus tea, chilled

¼ cup [25 g] dried goji berries

1¼ cups [165 g] frozen cubed cantaloupe

½ cup [120 g] plain whole-milk yogurt

1 Tbsp honey

Pinch of sea salt

This thick, shake-like smoothie has a flavor similar to melon candy with a slightly tart aftertaste, due to the antioxidant-rich goji berries and hibiscus tea. If you can't find hibiscus tea, feel free to replace with unsweetened cranberry juice; both have a deep red color and pucker-inducing tartness.

Make it

Place the hibiscus tea and goji berries in a blender and let soak for 10 minutes.

Add the cantaloupe, yogurt, honey, and salt. Start the blender on low speed and slowly increase to high speed. Blend until smooth and creamy.

Lychee Mango Freeze

1 cup [160 g] lychees, peeled, pitted, and frozen

¾ cup [105 g] frozen cubed mango

1 cup [240 g] plain whole-milk yogurt

1 tsp maple syrup

Pinch of sea salt

The tropical flavors and floral aromas of lychee and mango dominate this golden drink. A healthy amount of yogurt gives this blend a rich, creamy quality, with an added bonus of protein and gut-friendly probiotics.

Make it

Place the lychees, mango, yogurt, maple syrup, and salt in a blender. Start the blender on low speed and slowly increase to high speed. Blend until smooth and creamy.

RELAX

Magenta Dragon

1 cup [240 ml] plain unsweetened hemp milk

One 3½ oz [100 g] packet frozen dragon fruit (pitaya) purée

½ cup [85 g] frozen cubed mango

¼ cup [35 g] frozen banana slices

2 Tbsp hemp hearts

1 tsp agave syrup

Pinch of sea salt

This vibrant drink owes its magenta color to pitaya (also known as dragon fruit), which is an excellent source of heart-healthy omega-3 and omega-9 fatty acids. It's important to note that pitayas also come in white and yellow varieties, so while it's not essential to get the magenta one, you won't get that striking color with another variety.

Make it

Place the hemp milk, dragon fruit purée, mango, banana, hemp hearts, agave syrup, and salt in a blender. Start the blender on low speed and slowly increase to high speed. Blend until smooth and creamy.

Mango Turmeric Lassi

1¼ cups [175 g] frozen cubed mango

1 cup [240 g] plain Greek yogurt

½ cup [120 ml] carrot juice

1 Tbsp honey

½ tsp ground turmeric

¼ tsp freshly ground black pepper

⅛ tsp ground cardamom

Pinch of sea salt

RELAX

Inspired by the cooling Indian drink, this supercharged version has carrots and Greek yogurt added in for an extra dose of eye-friendly vitamin A, immunity-boosting vitamin C, and probiotics.

Make it

Place the mango, yogurt, carrot juice, honey, turmeric, pepper, cardamom, and salt in a blender. Start the blender on low speed and slowly increase to high speed. Blend until smooth and creamy.

Papaya Ginger Zen

1¼ cups [175 g] frozen diced papaya

1 golden kiwi, peeled, halved, and frozen

1 cup [240 ml] coconut milk beverage

2 tsp honey

1 tsp fresh lime juice

½ tsp grated fresh ginger

Pinch of sea salt

DIGESTION

The star ingredient in this smoothie is papaya, and rightly so: The fruit is a great source of vitamin C, fiber, potassium, and antioxidants. It also has an enzyme called papain that helps relieve stomach ailments.

Make it

Place the papaya, kiwi, coconut milk, honey, lime juice, ginger, and salt in a blender. Start the blender on low speed and slowly increase to high speed. Blend until smooth and creamy.

Piña Cauli-ada

1 cup [140 g] frozen pineapple chunks

½ cup [60 g] frozen riced cauliflower

½ cup [120 ml] coconut milk

2 pitted Medjool dates

1 tsp fresh lime juice

Pinch of sea salt

REPAIR

Do you like piña coladas? And getting lots of fiber? You're in luck because this smoothie satisfies both with a combination of pineapple, creamy canned coconut milk, and fiber- and vitamin K–rich cauliflower. Make sure to use pre-riced cauliflower rather than whole florets; the riced (or "grated") version makes it easier to incorporate.

Make it

Place the pineapple, cauliflower, coconut milk, dates, lime juice, salt, and ½ cup [120 ml] of water in a blender. Start the blender on low speed and slowly increase to high speed. Blend until smooth and creamy.

Cool Down

These super hydrating smoothies are filled with lots of healthy nutrients to help you repair your body after a workout or a stress-filled day.

Asian Pear Refresher

2 Tbsp raw cashews

1 Asian pear, cored and chopped

½ cup [85 g] cucumber slices

5 sprigs parsley

2 Tbsp hemp hearts

½ cup [120 ml] coconut water

1 tsp honey

Pinch of sea salt

Cashews and hemp hearts add protein and heart-healthy omega fatty acids to this clean and refreshing, just-sweet-enough smoothie. Crisp, juicy Asian pear and cucumber combine with potassium- and electrolyte-filled coconut water to make this a perfect post-workout drink. The skin is left on the Asian pear for added fiber, but feel free to peel the fruit if you prefer a silkier final texture. Note: You'll need to start this smoothie recipe the night before.

Make it

Place the cashews in a bowl with ½ cup [120 ml] of water. Cover and refrigerate overnight.

Drain the cashews and add to a blender along with the pear, cucumber, parsley, hemp hearts, coconut water, honey, and salt. Start the blender on low speed and slowly increase to high speed. Blend until smooth and creamy.

Fruit and Veg Green Smoothie

1 cup [150 g] diced cucumber

1 cup [25 g] packed chopped kale

1 cup [140 g] frozen pineapple chunks

½ cup [60 g] diced Granny Smith apple

2 tsp fresh lemon juice

1 tsp spirulina powder

Pinch of sea salt

REFRESH

This classic smoothie uses a special superfood to give it a major healthy boost: spirulina. This ultra-nutritious algae, blended up here with equal parts veggies and fruits, is ideal for when you need a refreshing boost to your day.

Make it

Place the cucumber, kale, pineapple, apple, lemon juice, spirulina, salt, and ¼ cup [60 ml] of water in a blender. Start the blender on low speed and slowly increase to high speed. Blend until smooth and creamy.

Green Hydration

1 cup [160 g] frozen seedless green grapes

1 cup [20 g] packed baby spinach

½ cup [85 g] cucumber slices

½ cup [60 g] chopped celery

½ cup [120 ml] coconut water

2 tsp fresh lemon juice

1 tsp maple syrup

Pinch of sea salt

REFRESH

A frothy green smoothie full of vitamin-rich, hydrating ingredients, this blend is excellent for helping with inflammation. A healthy amount of spinach adds lots of vitamins K, A, and C, while grapes are super hydrating.

Make it

Place the grapes, spinach, cucumber, celery, coconut water, lemon juice, maple syrup, and salt in a blender. Start the blender on low speed and slowly increase to high speed. Blend until smooth and creamy.

Honeydew Mint

1½ cups [225 g] frozen cubed honeydew

1 cup [240 ml] coconut water

2 tsp fresh lime juice

1 tsp honey

5 fresh mint leaves

Pinch of sea salt

REPAIR

Coconut water is the perfect remedy after an intense workout—high in electrolytes, potassium, sodium, and magnesium, all nutrients that help with rehydrating. A touch of mint gives this drink a bright scent and helps with upset stomachs.

Make it

Place the honeydew, coconut water, lime juice, honey, mint, and salt in a blender. Start the blender on low speed and slowly increase to high speed. Blend until smooth and creamy.

Minty Meyer Lemon Cooler

1¼ cups [200 g] frozen seedless green grapes

**1 cup [120 g] diced sweet red apple,
such as Fuji, Gala, or Honeycrisp**

½ cup [120 ml] fresh Meyer lemon juice

1 Tbsp fresh mint leaves

Pinch of sea salt

This frothy and refreshing drink is reminiscent of a tart Italian ice, with a lot more health benefits. Grapes can naturally reduce inflammation and are eyes' best friend. Use the sweetest grape variety you can find (we recommend Cotton Candy grapes; otherwise, you may need to add a few teaspoons of honey to taste).

Make it

Place the grapes, apple, lemon juice, mint, and salt in a blender. Start the blender on low speed and slowly increase to high speed. Blend until smooth and creamy.

REFRESH

Sweet Corn Shake

1½ cups [210 g] frozen corn kernels

1 cup [240 ml] whole milk

1 Tbsp honey

2 tsp bee pollen granules

Pinch of sea salt

REPAIR

Sweet and thick, this smoothie brings out the best flavor from summertime corn. For the highest sweetness, use fresh, in-season corn and cut off and freeze the kernels yourself; if that's not an option, use frozen corn kernels labeled "sweet" or "super sweet."

Make it Place the corn, milk, honey, bee pollen, and salt in a blender. Start the blender on low speed and slowly increase to high speed. Blend until smooth and creamy.

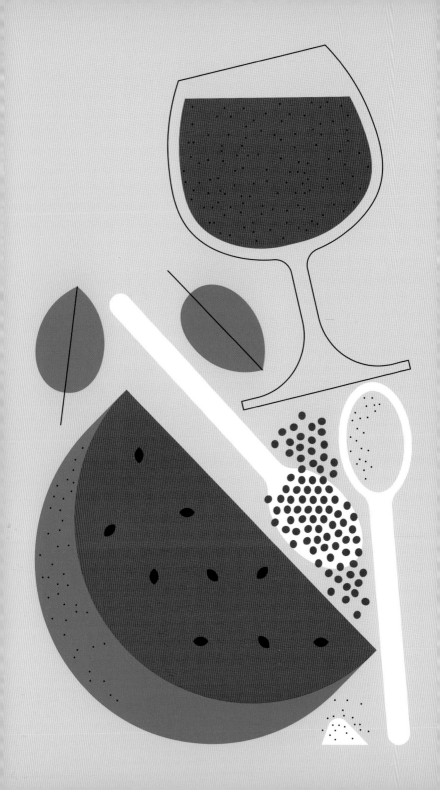

Watermelon Basil Slushie

1½ cups [225 g] frozen cubed watermelon

1½ cups [225 g] refrigerated cubed watermelon

1 Tbsp fresh lime juice

2 fresh basil leaves

Pinch of sea salt

2 Tbsp chia seeds

REFRESH

This thirst-quenching drink is ideal for a hot summer afternoon. Watermelon (which is naturally low in sugar and high in antioxidants) is 92 percent water, which creates a more slushie-like consistency.

Make it

Place the frozen and refrigerated watermelon cubes, lime juice, basil, and salt in a blender. Start the blender on low speed and slowly increase to high speed. Blend until smooth and creamy. Add the chia seeds and blend on medium speed to combine.

Sweet Treats

Decadent and rich, these healthy-ish smoothies are just what you need to treat yourself.

Black Forest Cherry Shake

1¼ cups [300 ml] plain unsweetened oat milk

1 cup [165 g] frozen pitted sweet cherries

¼ cup [30 g] cacao nibs

1 tsp maple syrup

⅛ tsp almond extract

Pinch of sea salt

If you ever need an excuse to have more chocolate in your life, this is it. Cacao nibs (made from crushed cacao beans, which are used to make chocolate) are packed with antioxidants, fiber, iron, and magnesium and can boost your mood.

Make it

Place the oat milk, cherries, cacao nibs, maple syrup, almond extract, and salt in a blender. Start the blender on low speed and slowly increase to high speed. Blend until smooth and creamy.

Blueberry Cheesecake

1½ cups [210 g] frozen blueberries

1 cup [235 g] whole-milk or low-fat cottage cheese

¼ cup [60 ml] whole milk

4 tsp honey

½ tsp fresh lemon zest

¼ tsp vanilla extract

HEARTY

Seriously—this tastes exactly like a blueberry cheese-cake in smoothie form. Much like its namesake, this drink is slightly tangy and just sweet enough, with a beautiful purple color. Unlike other recipes in this book, it doesn't need an added pinch of sea salt because cottage cheese already includes salt.

Make it

Place the blueberries, cottage cheese, milk, honey, lemon zest, and vanilla in a blender. Start the blender on low speed and slowly increase to high speed. Blend until smooth and creamy.

Persimmon Perfection

1½ cups [200 g] frozen diced ripe Fuyu persimmons

1 cup [240 ml] plain unsweetened oat milk

¼ cup [30 g] walnut pieces, toasted and cooled completely

½ tsp vanilla extract

⅛ tsp cinnamon

Pinch of ground cloves

Pinch of allspice

Pinch of sea salt

IMMUNITY

Creamy and custard-like, this smoothie owes its lightly sweet flavor entirely to persimmons. Be sure to use Fuyu persimmons (the squat-shaped, non-astringent variety) rather than Hachiya (the heart-shaped variety that needs to be fully ripe and soft before eating).

Make it

Place the persimmons, oat milk, walnuts, vanilla, cinnamon, cloves, allspice, and salt in a blender. Start the blender on low speed and slowly increase to high speed. Blend until smooth and creamy. Serve immediately.

Note: Due to the high pectin content of persimmons, this smoothie must be consumed right away. Otherwise, it will thicken into a spoonable rather than drinkable consistency.

TBD (Tahini-Banana-Date)

1 cup [240 ml] plain unsweetened oat milk

1 medium banana, peeled, sliced, and frozen

5 pitted Medjool dates

2 Tbsp tahini

$\frac{1}{8}$ tsp cinnamon

Pinch of nutmeg

Pinch of sea salt

ENERGY

A frozen banana, oat milk, and tahini stand in for vanilla ice cream and milk in this much-healthier, no-sugar-added, smoothie-fied version of the quintessential Palm Springs milkshake. Dates are naturally high in sugar, as well as a good source of fiber and potassium, so they are great for a quick energy boost.

Make it

Place the oat milk, banana, dates, tahini, cinnamon, nutmeg, and salt in a blender. Start the blender on low speed and slowly increase to high speed. Blend until smooth and creamy.

Frozen Black Sesame Soy Latte

½ cup [70 g] black sesame seeds, lightly toasted and cooled completely

1 cup [135 g] frozen banana slices

1 cup [240 ml] plain unsweetened soy milk

1 Tbsp maple syrup

Pinch of sea salt

HEARTY

Sesame seeds have a lot going for them for such a small seed: They are a good source not only of protein but also calcium, antioxidants, fiber, and healthy fats. Thanks to the addition of fibrous banana and protein-rich soy milk, this rich and nutty drink is super filling.

Make it

Place the sesame seeds in a blender. Blend on low speed for 5 seconds, then pulse until sandy in texture. Add the banana, soy milk, maple syrup, and salt. Start the blender on low speed and slowly increase to high speed. Blend until smooth and creamy.

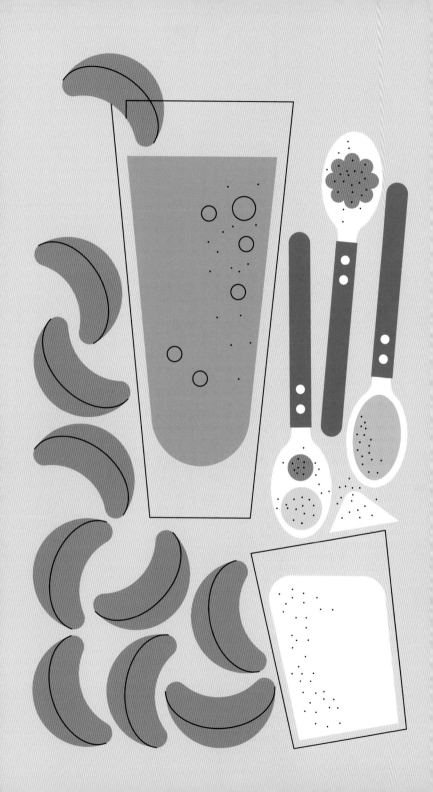

Grown-Up Orange Cream-Pop

1¼ cups [160 g] frozen tangerine segments

1 tsp finely grated tangerine zest

1 cup [240 g] plain whole-milk yogurt

1½ tsp honey

¼ tsp vanilla extract

⅛ tsp orange blossom water

Pinch of sea salt

MOOD

This nostalgic drink is a fancy version of the childhood frozen dessert. The tangerines are a great source of vitamin C and fiber, while the yogurt provides plenty of protein and calcium. The secret ingredient in this smoothie, however, is the orange blossom water, which is the by-product of distilling bitter orange blossoms into essential oil. In addition to imparting a delicate floral aroma, orange blossom water is known for its calming, stress-reducing, aromatherapeutic properties.

Make it

Place the tangerine segments, tangerine zest, yogurt, honey, vanilla, orange blossom water, and salt in a blender. Start the blender on low speed and slowly increase to high speed. Blend until smooth and creamy.

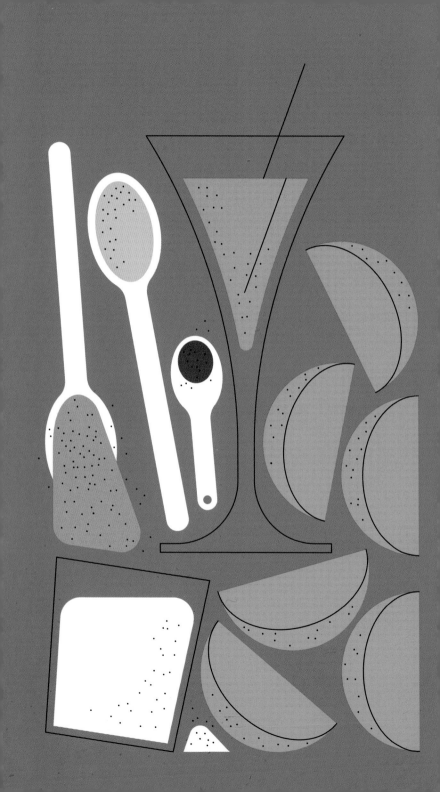

Peaches and Cream

1¼ cups [300 g] plain whole-milk yogurt

1 cup [140 g] frozen peach slices

2 Tbsp flaxseed meal

1 Tbsp honey

¼ tsp vanilla extract

Pinch of sea salt

IMMUNITY

Need a fruity dessert option that both tastes good and is good for you? Look no further than this protein- and antioxidant-rich smoothie. Flaxseed meal is the particular special ingredient here in that it contains fiber (good for your tummy), omega-3 fatty acids (heart-friendly), and lignans (cancer fighters).

Make it

Place the yogurt, peach slices, flaxseed meal, honey, vanilla, and salt in a blender. Start the blender on low speed and slowly increase to high speed. Blend until smooth and creamy.

Plum Perfection

1¼ cups [300 ml] plain unsweetened almond milk

1 cup [150 g] frozen red plum slices

5 pitted prunes

2 tsp honey

¼ tsp cinnamon

⅛ tsp almond extract

Pinch of sea salt

Plums and their dried versions, prunes, are an amazing source of fiber and key to healthy digestion. These dense fruits are given a sweet and light treatment with dashes of honey, cinnamon, and almond to create a dessert-like treat.

Make it

Place the almond milk, plums, prunes, honey, cinnamon, almond extract, and salt in a blender. Start the blender on low speed and slowly increase to high speed. Blend until smooth and creamy.

Pumpkin Spice Frappé

1 cup [240 ml] plain unsweetened almond milk

½ cup [130 g] canned pumpkin purée (not pumpkin pie filling), chilled

½ cup [70 g] frozen banana slices

¼ cup [35 g] unsalted pepitas, toasted and cooled completely

1 Tbsp maple syrup

¼ tsp cinnamon

⅛ tsp ground nutmeg

Pinch of sea salt

IMMUNITY

Let's be honest: Everyone has a soft spot for pumpkin spice. Comforting and sweet, it makes us think of cozy winter days. This smoothie hits all the right notes that a pumpkin pie does, just with the added bonus of it being healthy-ish!

Make it

Place the almond milk, pumpkin purée, banana, pepitas, maple syrup, cinnamon, nutmeg, and salt in a blender. Start the blender on low speed and slowly increase to high speed. Blend until smooth and creamy.

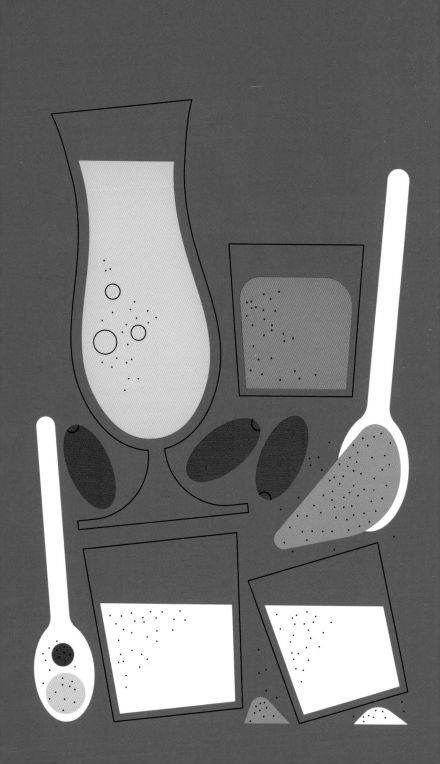

Sweetie Pie

1½ cups [360 ml] plain unsweetened almond milk

½ cup [125 g] frozen sweet potato purée

3 pitted Medjool dates

2 Tbsp flaxseed meal

¼ tsp grated fresh ginger

⅛ tsp cinnamon

Pinch of ground nutmeg

Pinch of sea salt

MEMORY

Perfect for a guilt-free holiday treat, this creamy smoothie is reminiscent of sweet potato pie, minus all the typical added sugar. As an extra bonus, sweet potatoes are high in fiber and a great source of beta-carotene, which can help with your cognitive functions.

Make it

Place the almond milk, sweet potato purée, dates, flaxseed meal, ginger, cinnamon, nutmeg, and salt in a blender. Start the blender on low speed and slowly increase to high speed. Blend until smooth and creamy.

Index